**Aberdeenshire**
COUNCIL

Aberdeenshire Libraries
www.aberdeenshire.gov.uk/libraries
Renewals Hotline 01224 661511

2 8 JAN 2016

HQ

First
Facts

Water in Our World

# Cleaning Water

by Rebecca Olien

raintree

Raintree is an imprint of Capstone Global Library Limited, a company incorporated in England and Wales having its registered office at 264 Banbury Road, Oxford, OX2 7DY – Registered company number: 6695582
**www.raintree.co.uk**
myorders@raintree.co.uk

**Editorial Credits**
Abby Colich, editor; Kyle Grenz, designer; Wanda Winch, media researcher; Laura Manthe, production specialist

**Photo Credits**
Capstone, 16-17; Dreamstime: Luckydoor, 13, Izanbar, 10, Nostal6ie, 1, Presse750, 19; Shutterstock: AuntSpray, 7, Chaiyapruk Chanwatthana, 9, 15, daizuxion, 20, Ecelop, wave design, Kekyalyayan, cover, 1, KPG Payless2, 5, tachygossus, splash design

ISBN 978-1-4747-1223-1
19  18  17  16  15
10 9 8 7 6 5 4 3 2 1

**British Library Cataloguing in Publication Data**
A full catalogue record for this book is available from the British Library.

Every effort has been made to contact copyright holders of material reproduced in this book. Any omissions will be rectified in subsequent printings if notice is given to the publisher.

All the Internet addresses (URLs) given in this book were valid at the time of going to press. However, due to the dynamic nature of the Internet, some addresses may have changed, or sites may have changed or ceased to exist since publication. While the author and publisher regret any inconvenience this may cause readers, no responsibility for any such changes can be accepted by either the author or the publisher.

Printed in China.

# Contents

# To the tap

Turn on the tap and clear, clean water rushes out. People drink millions of glasses of clean water every day. Getting clean water to the tap is a long process. Water goes through many stages of cleaning before people can drink it.

# Water sources

The water people drink comes from different sources. In many areas, people get water from rivers and lakes.

Some water seeps into the ground. It collects in underground *aquifers*. In some places, people dig wells to reach *groundwater*.

**aquifer**—an underground lake
**groundwater**—water that is found under ground

GROUNDWATER AQUIFER

**toxin**—poison
**filter**—a device that cleans liquids or gases as they pass through it

7

The water in rivers and lakes is not safe for people to drink. Rain washes dirt and waste into rivers. Waste from homes and farms *pollute* water sources.

*Water treatment works* clean water and make it safe to drink. Dirt and other *particles* are taken out of the water. *Bacteria* that could make people ill are also killed.

**pollute**—to make something dirty or unsafe
**water treatment works**—a place where water is cleaned for people to use at home
**particle**—a tiny piece of something
**bacteria**—very small living things; some bacteria cause disease

Before water is treated, it must be pumped from a lake or river. Pumps also bring water up from under ground.

Pumps push water through miles of large pipes. The pipes carry water to tanks in water treatment works.

## Fact!

*Reservoirs* are often built to store drinking water. The water is cleaned and moved to buildings from the reservoir.

**reservoir**—an artificial lake where water is collected

Water treatment works take out *sediment*. Sediment is made up of dirt and particles found in water. A powder called alum is added to the water. Alum makes the particles sticky. The sticky particles sink to the bottom of the tanks. Cleaner water is left at the top. This water is then pushed through filters to take out any remaining particles.

sediment—bits of sand or clay carried by water or wind

This machine is removing sediment from water.

# Disinfection

*Disinfection* is the next step in making water clean. Treatment works disinfect water by adding *chemicals* that kill bacteria.

Most treatment works add chlorine or chloramine the to water. Treating water with these chemicals helps protect people from disease.

**disinfection**—a process that kills harmful germs
**chemical**—a substance that creates a reaction; chlorine is a chemical used to treat water

**Fact!**

Chlorine is added to swimming pools to keep the water clean.

In this part of a treatment works, chemicals are added to the water.

# Moving water

Once it is treated, the water is ready for people to use. Clean water is pumped from the treatment works to storage tanks. In some places, water can be stored in large towers.

## Cleaning water

**source water**

Water is pumped to the treatment works.

**removing sediment**

Alum is added. Sediment sinks to the bottom of the tank.

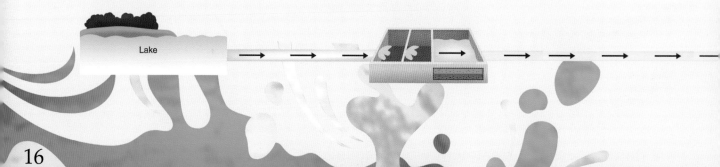

Lake

Water flows from storage tanks through underground pipes called mains. Large water mains connect to smaller pipes. These pipes carry clean water to homes, schools and businesses.

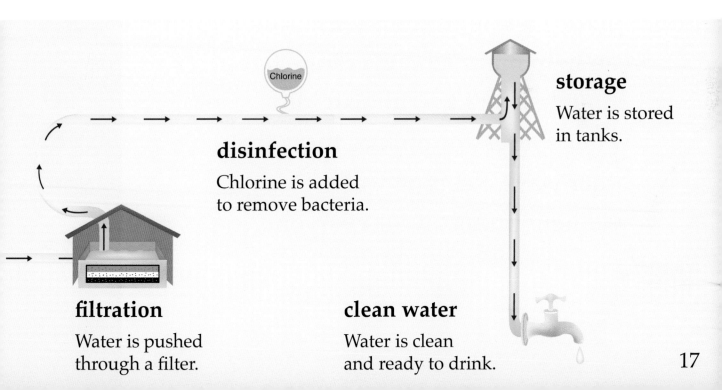

**storage**
Water is stored in tanks.

Chlorine

**disinfection**
Chlorine is added to remove bacteria.

**filtration**
Water is pushed through a filter.

**clean water**
Water is clean and ready to drink.

# Clean water

People need clean water to drink, cook and bathe. In some parts of the world, people don't have enough clean water. Dirty water can cause illness.

Don't waste water. Saving water can help make sure everyone has enough. Don't tip rubbish into water sources or pollute them in other ways. Keeping water clean will help protect it for everyone.

**Fact!**

Every year, 3.4 million people die from diseases caused by unclean drinking water.

# Amazing but true!

Plants help keep water clean. Some plants grow in wetlands. Particles stick to plant roots and settle into the dirt. Water is cleaned as it flows through layers of roots and dirt.

# Hands on: cleaning water

Water treatment works remove sediment from water with alum. This experiment will show you how alum works.

## What you need

- 240 ml cold water
- clear jar
- 1/2 teaspoon ground coffee
- 1 teaspoon flour

## What you do

1. Pour the cold water into the clear jar.
2. Add the ground coffee.
3. Look at the side of the jar. Notice how the coffee floats on the surface of the water.
4. Sprinkle the flour into the jar.
5. Look through the side of the jar to see what happens. The flour will form little clumps. As the clumps get heavier, they will fall to the bottom of the jar, bringing coffee grounds with them. Alum works the same way in a water tank. Particles of dirt stick to the alum. The particles sink to the bottom of the tank.

# Glossary

**aquifer**—an underground lake

**bacteria**—very small living things; some bacteria cause disease

**chemical**—a substance that creates a reaction; chlorine is a chemical used to treat water

**disinfection**—a process that kills harmful germs

**filter**—a device that cleans liquids or gases as they pass through it

**groundwater**—water that is found under ground

**particle**—a tiny piece of something

**pollute**—to make something dirty or unsafe

**reservoir**—an artificial lake where water is collected

**sediment**—bits of sand or clay carried by water or wind

**toxin**—poison

**water treatment works**—a place where water is cleaned for people to use at home

# Read more

*Every Last Drop: Bringing Clean Water Home*, Michelle Mulder (Orca Book Publishers, 2014)

*Water* (How Does My Home Work?), Chris Oxlade (Heinemann, 2013)

*You Wouldn't Want to Live Without Clean Water!* (You Wouldn't Want To), Roger Canavan (Franklin Watts, 2015)

# Websites

**Water facts**
http://www.sciencekids.co.nz/sciencefacts/water.html

**The water family water conservation game**
http://www.thewaterfamily.co.uk/

**The Water Education Foundation water facts for kids**
http://www.watereducation.org/water-kids

# Comprehension questions

1. Why shouldn't people dump waste in water sources or pollute them in other ways?
2. What would happen if there were no water treatment works on Earth? How would life be different for people?
3. Reread pages 6 and 7. Compare and contrast how water gets from wells to people's homes and how water gets from lakes and rivers to people's homes.

# Index